The Tree Lady

THE TRUE STORY OF HOW ONE
TREE-LOVING WOMAN CHANGED A CITY FOREVER

H. Joseph Hopkins

illustrated by Jill McElmurry

Beach Lane Books • NEW YORK   LONDON   TORONTO   SYDNEY   NEW DELHI

KATHERINE OLIVIA SESSIONS grew up in the woods of

Northern California. She gathered leaves from oaks and elms. She collected needles from pines and redwoods. And she braided them together with flowers to make necklaces and bracelets.

It was the 1860s, and girls from Kate's side of town weren't supposed to get their hands dirty.

But Kate did.

Kate listened well in school. She learned how to write and count. She remembered the poems and stories she read. But best of all, she liked studying wind and rain, muscles and bones, plants and trees. Especially trees.

Most girls were discouraged from studying science.

But not Kate.

Kate felt the trees were her friends. She loved the way they reached toward the sky and how their branches stretched wide to catch the light. Trees seemed to Kate like giant umbrellas that sheltered her and the animals, birds, and plants that lived in the forest.

Not everyone feels at home in the woods.

But Kate did.

When Kate grew up, she left home to study science at college. She looked at soil and insects through a microscope. She learned how plants made food and how they drank water. And she studied trees from around the world.

No woman had ever graduated from the University of California with a degree in science.

But in 1881, Kate did.

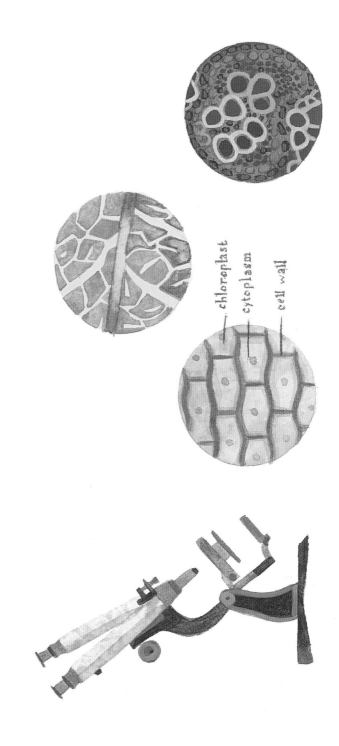

chloroplast
cytoplasm
cell wall

After graduation, Kate took a job in Southern California. When her boat docked in San Diego, she saw that her new home was a desert town. Kate never thought she would live in a place with very few trees.

But now she did.

Kate began her job as a teacher. She was also the vice principal of the school, so she had to make sure that everyone followed the rules.

Kate missed studying science and was not sure she would stay on the job.

But for two years, she did.

From her school, Kate could see City Park in the hills above town. It was called a park, but it didn't look like one. It was where people grazed cattle and dumped garbage.

Most San Diegans didn't think trees could ever grow there.

But Kate did.

With Kate's love for the woods, she thought San Diego needed trees more than anything else. So she left teaching to become a gardener. She knew she must plant trees that could live in dry soil with lots and lots of sunshine.

Her friends worried Kate wouldn't find trees like that.

But she did.

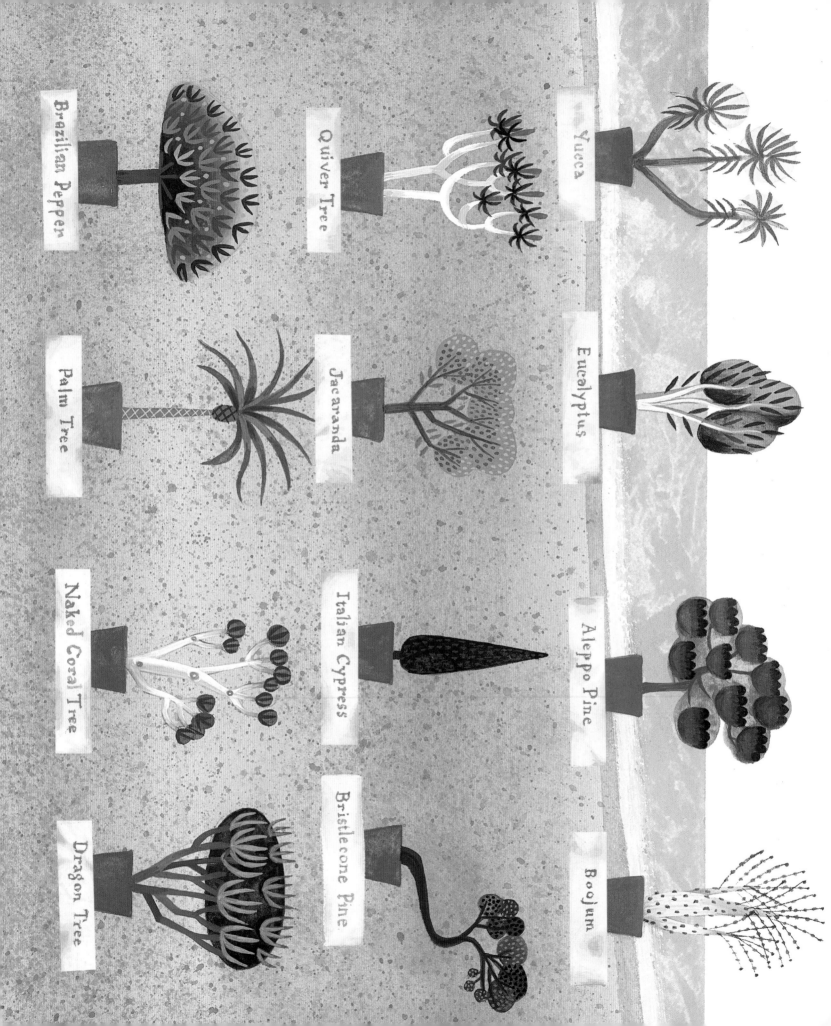

Kate became a tree hunter. She wrote letters to gardeners all over the world and asked them to send her seeds that could grow in a desert. She also traveled south into Mexico to look for trees that liked hot, dry weather and steep hills and canyons.

Not everyone knows how to hunt for trees.

But Kate did.

Soon Kate's trees were planted along streets, around schools, and in small parks and plazas all over town. People bought trees from Kate's nursery and planted them in their yards.

From elms and oaks to eucalyptuses and palms, by the turn of the century, young trees from Kate's nursery were growing in every part of San Diego.

Most people didn't think a desert town could sustain so many trees.

But Kate did.

Then in 1909, the city leaders announced that a great fair called the Panama-California Exposition was coming to San Diego in 1915. The fair would be held in City Park, which was now called Balboa Park. Kate felt Balboa Park still needed more trees—thousands more—to look beautiful and to shade the visitors that came to the fair.

That was too many trees for Kate to plant by herself, but she knew lots of people could do it together. She asked her friends to bring their friends and come to the park for tree-planting parties. Again and again, people volunteered to help.

Those volunteers weren't sure they could plant enough trees.

But before long, they did.

And when the fair opened, San Diego was ready. Millions of trees and plants filled Balboa Park. The fair had so many visitors, it stayed open for two years instead of one. People came from near and far to see the attractions and stroll in the cool shade.

The fairgoers couldn't believe San Diego had such magnificent gardens.

But thanks to Kate, it did.

In the years after the fair, Kate was given many awards for her work, and people took to calling her the Mother of Balboa Park. She continued gardening and planting trees until her death in 1940.

Back then, few could have imagined that San Diego would become the lush, leafy city it is today.

But all along, year after year, Katherine Olivia Sessions did.

Author's note

WHEN KATE SESSIONS CAME TO SAN DIEGO IN 1883, she discovered drought-resistant native plants flourishing in the region's Mediterranean climate. She also found nonnative tropical plants, such as poinsettia and bougainvillea, growing outdoors under the city's sunny skies. Kate saw that the landscape, running as it does from the seashore to the mountains and farther east into the desert, included many subclimates. This made the area perfect for growing a great variety of trees and plants. Yet San Diego's City Park was dry, dusty, and all but barren. Kate wanted to change that.

In 1892 Kate made a deal with city leaders to use land in City Park for a plant nursery. In exchange, she promised to plant one hundred trees in the park every year and give the city three hundred more trees for planting in other places. People loved Kate's trees, and by the early 1900s, one in four trees growing in San Diego came from her nursery.

Though Kate is most celebrated for her work in City Park, which was later renamed Balboa Park, she wasn't just interested in big projects like the Panama-California Exposition. Kate wanted *everyone* to be successful in the garden. For more than forty years, she wrote newspaper and magazine articles that introduced plants and explained how to care for them. And for decades she played a leading role in the San Diego Floral Association's monthly meetings, where she was loved for her sparkling, witty, and encouraging answers to gardeners' questions.

In 1939, just a year before she died, eighty-two-year-old Kate attended a festive luncheon—a "fussy doodle" as she called such affairs—where she was the first woman to receive the Meyer Medal, an award given for exemplary service to horticultural science.

Kate received many honors during her lifetime, but the one that pleased her most was being called the Mother of Balboa Park. Thanks to Kate, the park has come a long way from its humble beginnings. Today it remains a haven for the people of San Diego and for the fourteen million visitors who come each year to enjoy its enormous variety of trees, shrubs, flowers, and vines.

To my favorite trees of New Mexico,
the mighty cottonwood and the graceful aspen —J. M.

To Eunice, Lori, and Wade,
for happy hours with children's books—H. J. H.

Thank you to Emily Watkins for lending a hand.—J. M.

Special thanks to my editor Andrea Welch; to the faculty and students of the beach-front book conference where this story was first written down; to the San Diego History Center, the San Diego Natural History Museum, the San Diego Public Library California Room, and the San Diego Floral Association; to Nancy Carol Carter of the University of San Diego School of Law; and to Elizabeth C. MacPhail for her book *Kate Sessions: Pioneer Horticulturist*. For more information about Kate Sessions, please visit sandiegohistory.org/bio/sessions/sessions.htm.—H. J. H.

BEACH LANE BOOKS • An imprint of Simon & Schuster Children's Publishing Division • 1230 Avenue of the Americas, New York, New York 10020 • Text copyright © 2013 by H. Joseph Hopkins • Illustrations copyright © 2013 by Jill McElmurry • All rights reserved, including the right of reproduction in whole or in part in any form. BEACH LANE BOOKS is a trademark of Simon & Schuster, Inc. • For information about special discounts for bulk purchases, please contact Simon & Schuster Special Sales at 1-866-506-1949 or business@simonandschuster.com. • The Simon & Schuster Speakers Bureau can bring authors to your live event. For more information or to book an event, contact the Simon & Schuster Speakers Bureau at 1-866-248-3049 or visit our website at www.simonspeakers.com. • Book design by Lauren Rille • The text for this book is set in Andrade. • The illustrations for this book are rendered in gouache on 140 lb. cold-pressed watercolor paper. • Manufactured in China 0117 SCP 10 9 8 7 6 • Library of Congress Cataloging-in-Publication Data • Hopkins, H. Joseph. • The tree lady : the true story of how one tree-loving woman changed a city forever / H. Joseph Hopkins ; illustrated by Jill McElmurry. —p. cm. • ISBN 978-1-4424-1402-0 (hardcover) • ISBN 978-1-4424-8727-7 (eBook) • 1. Sessions, Kate Olivia, 1857–1940—Juvenile literature. • H. Joseph Hopkins ; illustrated by Jill McElmurry. Jill, illustrator. II. Title. • SB63.S47.HD • 635.092—dc23 • [B] • 2012032903